To all the mums and dads
of all the little boys and girls —
love them,
support them,
acknowledge them.

Greg ♡

Text copyright © 2023 by Greg Vlant
Illustrations copyright © 2024 by Evgenia Malina

All rights reserved. No parts of this book may be reproduced or transmitted in any form or by any means, electronic or mechanical, including photocopying, recording, or by any information storage and retrieval system, without prior written permission from the author.

For permission requests (other than for review purposes),
please contact gregvlant@gmail.com

First Edition: May 2024, Printed in Australia

ISBN 978-1-7635264-0-2

Greg Vlant

Master Of The Shoe

Illustrated by Evgenia Malina

Here's little Timmy, and he's only 3.
There are a lot of things he is capable of,
I'm sure you will agree.

He can do his pees,
and he can do a poo.
Now on to the next challenge
that Timmy must get through.

He loves it when his mummy helps him.
He loves it when his daddy helps him too.
Little Timmy is a big boy now,
and he wants to master the shoe.

He put on his top, and pulled up his pants.
"Shoes! Shoes!" He yelled with a dance.
His socks went on. No problem at all.
Next up? His shoes, 3 pairs in his drawer.

Pulling it open, eager to give it a go.
Boys and girls get ready,
FOR THE SHOW!

Timmy picked up his shoe,
looked them right in the eye.

Whispered softly, "There's no need to cry."

"Timmy, Timmy, please don't wear us.
Don't rush any decisions.
It's something we can discuss."

A shiny black pair, a pair he named Klute.
Jumped out of his hands and gave him the boot.

These were sneakers, he named them Gruff.

"I'm going to get these on, I've had enough! Time for some magic. Abracadabra! Alakazam!"

A whoosh and a poof, but the sneakers yelled, "SCRAAAM!"

Timmy thought, "What am I doing wrong?
Hold up. Wait a minute.
What if I sing them a song?"

"Twinkle, twinkle, little shoes,
How I wonder why you refuse.
On my feet, feeling so high.
Come on shoes, let's give it a try!"

It was worth a shot. A shot that didn't go far.
But when a challenge confronts Timmy, he's not afraid to spar.

With determination in his corner, and his mouthguard in.
The battle was on, Timmy for the win.

Pair number 3. Undefeated kicks.
They had been there before and knew all the tricks.

A bob and a weave. A slip and a roll.
The kicks had moves, but Timmy was taking control.

The bell rang for round 2, round 3, then round 4.
Timmy ahead, settling the score.

The kicks were tired, it was their time to give in.
"Let's work together," Timmy said with a grin.

He lined his toes up with the hole.
Pushed his foot in with a slight roll.
All the way in until his heel hit the back.
Now it's time for YOU, to give it a crack.

"I did it! I did it!" He got them on.
He kept going, feeling strong!
He kept them on, splashing in a puddle.
Mummy and daddy - a kiss and a cuddle.

Timmy has now become Master of the shoe.
He never gave up and neither should you!

www.ingramcontent.com/pod-product-compliance
Lightning Source LLC
Chambersburg PA
CBHW041528070526
44585CB00003B/123